SIKHISM

GLOBAL CITIZENS: WORLD RELIGIONS

Published in the United States of America by Cherry Lake Publishing
Ann Arbor, Michigan
www.cherrylakepublishing.com

Content Adviser: Sikh Society of Michigan

Reading Adviser: Marla Conn MS, Ed., Literacy specialist, Read-Ability, Inc.

Photo Credits: © szefei/Shutterstock, cover, 1, 6; © Infinite Graphics/Shutterstock, 5; © Karve/Shutterstock, 8; © pandora64/Shutterstock, 10; © Serban Bogdan/Shutterstock, 13; © Fat Jackey/Shutterstock, 14; © saiko3p/Shutterstock, 16; © Dima Fadeev/Shutterstock, 19; © Anton_Ivanov/Shutterstock, 21; © reddees/Shutterstock, 22; © Dmitry Kalinovsky/Shutterstock, 24; © northallerton/Shutterstock, 26; © Don Mammoser/Shutterstock, 27; © India Picture/Shutterstock, 28

Library of Congress Cataloging-in-Publication Data on file.

Cherry Lake Publishing would like to acknowledge the work of the Partnership for 21st Century Learning.
Please visit *www.p21.org* for more information.

Printed in the United States of America
Corporate Graphics

ABOUT THE AUTHOR

Katie Marsico is the author of more than 200 children's books. She lives in a suburb of Chicago, Illinois, with her husband and children.

TABLE OF CONTENTS

History: Roots of the Religion

Since people began recording history, they have written about the idea of a power greater than themselves. Thousands of years later, various beliefs in this power continue to shape both individual lives and entire cultures. Religion is the system people use to organize such beliefs, as well as faith traditions and rules for worship.

How Sikhism Was Started

Sikhism is an example of a major world religion. It is monotheistic, or based on the idea that there is only one true God. Sikhs, or people who practice Sikhism, focus on performing good **deeds** as a way to love humanity. They believe this is a more important part of their faith than forcing members to observe strict religious **rituals**. One of their main goals is to

Guru Nanak was the founder of Sikhism.

always keep God in their heart and mind. Other goals involve demonstrating honesty, hard work, **equality**, generosity, and service. They try to earn honest livings, and always share with the needy.

The history of Sikhism traces back to Punjab. Hundreds of years ago, this region was made up of what are now northern India and Pakistan. Historians say Sikhism developed in Punjab in about 1500 CE. It was founded by Nanak, who lived from 1469 to 1539.

Nanak was born into a family that practiced **Hinduism**, but he rejected it. He also studied other religions, including **Islam**.

In Sikhism, all people have the chance to form a relationship with God.

Yet he questioned—and often opposed—some of these religions' ideas and habits. For example, Nanak disapproved of the caste system that existed within Hinduism. This system ranked people into different social classes, or groups. Those in the bottom classes often did not have the same rights and privileges as those at the top. Nanak also criticized how in some religions, rituals such as **fasting** and **pilgrimages** were religious requirements.

According to Nanak, everyone is equal in God's eyes. In addition, he taught that all people had the ability to form a relationship with God. Nanak said that this relationship didn't depend on social rankings and forced religious rituals.

A Period of Persecution

Eventually, Nanak was known as "Guru Nanak." A guru is a spiritual leader and teacher. Within Sikhism, gurus typically named a successor, or a person to follow them. Nine other gurus came after Guru Nanak between the 16th and early 18th centuries. During this period, Guru Arjan—the fifth Sikh guru—compiled scriptures, or holy writings, called the *Guru Granth Sahib*. Before

Developing Questions

Why did members of other religious groups—such as Muslims and Hindus—see Sikhism as a threat? Why does religious persecution ever occur? What specific Sikh beliefs did Muslims and Hindus disagree with? What connection existed between religion and politics when Sikhism first developed in Punjab?

The first two questions are compelling questions. They don't have straightforward answers. Yet compelling questions often trigger interesting discussions and debates. Meanwhile, the third and fourth questions are supporting questions. They have more clear-cut answers and are often used to form responses to compelling questions.

The *Guru Granth Sahib* is the spiritual book of Sikhism.

his death, the last human Guru of the Sikhs ordained that from now on, *Guru Granth Sahib* would be their spiritual guide.

As Sikhism developed, members often faced persecution, or poor treatment, from people who disagreed with their faith. To many Sikhs, their religion was based on several of the same ideas as Islam and Hinduism. Yet Muslims, or followers of Islam, and Hindus didn't support the Sikhs' new "version" of their religious beliefs. Guru Arjan was working on the *Guru Granth Sahib* in 1606. He refused to give up his faith, and was tortured and killed for it. He became a martyr, or someone who dies for what they believe.

In order to defend themselves, the Sikhs organized a military force. They sometimes even waged battle against their **oppressors**. Nevertheless, they continued to experience persecution, and their ninth guru—Guru Tegh Bahadur—was also martyred. He wanted to protect the right of people to practice whatever faith they wanted. He believed strongly in human rights and the freedom of religion.

The Creation of the Khalsa

Guru Gobind Singh was the 10th and final human guru in Sikhism. In 1699, he took steps to formalize Guru Nanak's idea of Sikhs being a group of soldier-like **saints**. This new order was

Sikh Scriptures

The Guru Granth Sahib is a collection of 5,864 verses of hymns, or religious songs, and prayers, written in classical musical measures. The 1,430 pages of writings are based on the words and teachings of Sikh gurus and saints. They also contain several writings by Muslim and Hindu saints that Guru Arjan believed reflected the spirit of Sikhism. The Guru Granth Sahib contains various languages, including Punjabi and Gurmukhi.

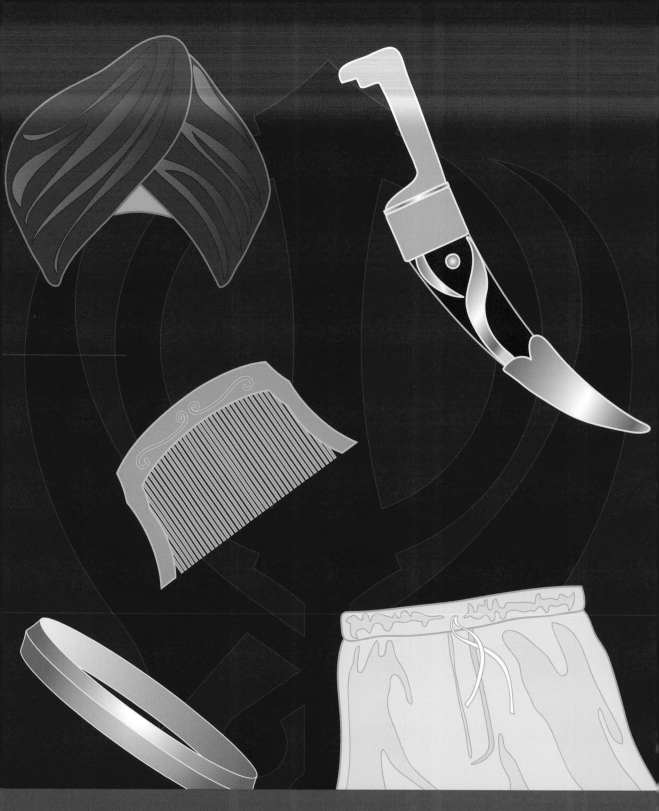

Khalsa members incorporate the Five Ks into their daily clothing.

called the Khalsa Panth, or the Community of the Pure. By joining, people demonstrate their total dedication to living according to the Guru's wisdom.

Members of the Khalsa observe the Five Ks. These physical symbols unify them, or join them together. They are *kesh* (uncut hair), *kanga* (a wooden comb), *kara* (a steel bracelet), *kacchera* (cotton undergarments), and *kirpan* (a sword). The first four Ks symbolize holiness, cleanliness, an ongoing connection to God, and self-control. In modern times, the kirpan is not used as a weapon. Instead, it is a reminder of the Sikhs' struggle against injustice.

Sikhs who have entered the Khalsa also wear a tied turban. This is a long cloth that is wound around their head to cover their hair, and is mostly worn by men. Women are not required to wear a turban, but some do. In Sikhism, the turban is a symbol of **dignity**, self-esteem, and royalty.

Geography: Mapping How Faith Formed

In 1799, a Sikh named Ranjit Singh established the Sikh Empire. He was a maharaja, or Indian prince, who ruled over Punjab. In Ranjit Singh's kingdom, more people practiced Hinduism and Islam than Sikhism. Yet the Sikhs were still able to celebrate their faith. While it lasted, the Sikh Empire was known for religious tolerance, or acceptance.

In 1839, however, Ranjit Singh died, and the empire he had built began to fall apart. Power struggles over who should follow him and the arrival of British colonists shaped much of the 1840s. By 1849, British troops had conquered Sikh forces and gained control of Punjab.

After 1849, both the British and Sikhs developed what was often a positive relationship. In several cases, Sikhs even became respected

Sikhism originated in India.

This sculpture is a memorial for the hundreds of Sikhs murdered in 1919.

soldiers in the British Army (and later, many served in World Wars One and Two). In 1919, though, a British general ordered the massacre, or mass killing, of Indians in Punjab. Hundreds of people died during the Amritsar massacre. In the years ahead, Indians pushed much harder to be free from British rule.

Issues Following Indian Independence

During the late 1940s, India achieved independence, or freedom, from Great Britain. Along the way, the area that was once considered India was divided into two separate nations—India and Pakistan. For the most part, Muslims settled in Pakistan, and Hindus relocated to India.

The question of where Sikhs fit into this arrangement was the source of conflict. Some stayed in Pakistan, others decided to live in India, and others moved to Europe and North America. Many Sikhs who remained in their homeland were determined to create

Gathering and Evaluating Sources

Reference books are valuable sources of information on Sikhism. But there are many ways to research Sikh culture. One is to study Sikh scriptures. Another is to actually spend time in a Sikh house of worship. Members of all religions are welcome to visit! If you have the opportunity to see a Sikh temple, pay attention to the architecture and design. Respectfully observe the customs of people celebrating their faith there. What do you notice? What do your observations reveal about Sikhism? How is this type of research similar to reading a book? How is it different? Why is it important to use multiple sources when studying any major world religion?

The Golden Temple, in Amritsar, is the most famous Sikh place of worship.

their own independent state. Sikhs felt they did not get fair treatment compared to people of other faiths, and they wanted this to change.

In 1966, the Indian government split Punjab into three parts and told the Sikhs they would control one. Nevertheless, many Sikhs said they were still being treated unfairly. In particular, they argued against the boundaries that Indian officials had set when they divided Punjab. Political tension and, ultimately, **pogroms** by the government killed many Sikhs during the next several decades.

Present Sikh Populations

Despite centuries of religious persecution, about 25 million people practice Sikhism today. It is the world's fifth most popular religion. More than 90 percent of Sikhs live in India. Other large groups are found in the United Kingdom, the United States, and Canada.

A Dazzling Sikh Holy Site

To Sikhs, the Golden Temple is one of the holiest sites in their religion. This house of worship is located in the city of Amritsar in northwestern Punjab. Guru Nanak lived in the area, though the temple itself was constructed during the time of Guru Arjan. Throughout the next few centuries, Muslims destroyed the building more than once. Yet Sikhs always rebuilt it, and it stands today. The temple reflects both Muslim and Hindu architecture and is decorated with marble, gold, and many precious stones.

CHAPTER 3

Civics: Organization and Ideas

All Sikhs are united by certain shared beliefs. These include faith in one God and the idea that good works are more important than certain religious rituals. Sikhs also say that humans experience a cycle of birth, death, and rebirth, or reincarnation. They think that when someone is reincarnated, his or her soul is reborn into a different body.

In Sikhism, karma, or a person's life force, affects the quality of his or her next existence. Good deeds lead to good karma, while evil actions create bad karma. According to Sikhs, the only way to break the cycle of birth, death, and rebirth is to achieve *mukti*. This is a state in which someone has complete union with God, even though they believe they can never have complete knowledge of him. Sikhs believe that people are able to become closer to God

Sikhs often pray in order to get closer to God.

through prayer, honest work, and giving to others. They also say that, to understand God better, it's necessary to avoid **vices** such as greed and anger. But they don't believe there is any system of heaven and hell. They believe it's possible to get closer to God during one's lifetime.

The Ways Sikhs Worship

When Sikhs worship, they do not rely on statues or **icons**. In addition, Sikh worship is not led by priests. Instead, *granthis* act as spiritual leaders within a *sangat*, or Sikh **congregation**. The sangat members can also lead services. Granthis read from scripture and perform initiation ceremonies, weddings, and funerals.

Sikh worship often takes place in a Sikh temple called a *gurdwara*. Before entering a gurdwara, Sikhs remove their shoes as a sign of respect. They also wash their hands and sometimes even their feet for similar reasons. People who aren't already wearing a turban are required to cover their heads. To further demonstrate their **reverence**, Sikhs bow down and touch the floor as they approach the *Guru Granth Sahib*.

Developing Claims and Using Evidence

In Sikhism, Amrit Sanskar is an initiation ceremony. Sikhs participate in it when they are ready to enter the Khalsa. Why do you think a special ceremony is required to join the Khalsa? Before responding, recall what the Khalsa represents in Sikhism. Also consider whether similar ceremonies exist in other religions and why they occur. Next, make a claim that answers the question above and find facts to support it. The library, Internet, and local gurdwaras are all good places to carry out your research! (Hint: Be careful when reviewing information online. Not every Web site is up-to-date or contains accurate details. For the most part, sites run by government agencies and colleges and universities are fairly reliable.)

People have to cover their heads before entering a gurdwara.

"Gatka" is a form of Sikh martial arts, which is demonstrated here during the Vaisakhi festival.

During worship, men and women generally sit on opposite sides of the gurdwara. Services typically include hymns (in the style of Indian classical music), readings from the *Guru Granth Sahib*, and a community meal. Members of a sanghat prepare food in the *langar*, which is an on-site community kitchen. These meals are open to people of all faiths. At the Golden Temple, up to 100,000 people eat there every day, free of charge.

Sikhs worship at home, as well. They are expected to say certain prayers in the morning, evening, and just before bed. When Sikhs pray, they believe they are spending time with God. To them,

Celebrating Faith

In Sikhism, several holidays and festivals serve as opportunities for people to celebrate their beliefs. Some of the main Sikh holy days are described below.

Holiday	When It's Celebrated	Main Theme
Gurpurbs	Throughout the year	Festivals celebrating various life events related to the Sikh gurus, including births and, in some cases, martyrdoms
Diwali (Festival of Light)	October and/or November	Celebration that lasts up to five days and remembers the release of Guru Hargobind from prison in 1619
Hola Mahalla	Mid-March	Festival that was at one time focused on the practice of Sikh military exercises but that now features martial arts parades, poetry readings, and music
Vaisakhi (Harvest Festival)	April 13 or April 14	The most important festival in Sikhism, a celebration that recalls Guru Gobind Singh forming the Khalsa in 1699

Note: Dates often vary, depending on the geographic location of individual faith communities and the practices within different denominations.

Most Sikh men wear turbans, and some women do too.

prayer is an opportunity to reach out to a mysterious being who is
both loving and powerful.

Similar but Not Always Identical

Just like in any religion, not all Sikhs choose to practice their
faith the same way. For example, even though keeping one's hair
uncut is an essential part of the religion, many followers decide to
cut their hair or shave their beards. In addition, not every Sikh
strictly follows the Five Ks when dressing in formal religious attire,
or clothing. Also, not all Sikhs undergo initiation ceremonies.

CHAPTER 4

Economics: Funding a Faith

Every religion depends on the faith of its members to survive. Yet most—including Sikhism—also require some level of financial support. Sikhs, for example, must address expenses for the construction and care of gurdwaras. Other costs involve the wide range of activities that occur within these houses of worship. Gurdwaras are the site of religious education classes, as well as community meals. Langars provide food to visitors of all religious backgrounds, not just members of Sikhism.

Since good works and giving are such important ideas within Sikhism, Sikhs are involved in many charitable activities. They feed the hungry and aid victims of natural disasters. They also assist the elderly and fund medical care for people who need surgeries and other treatments.

Khalsa Aid helped people affected by the floods in the United Kingdom in 2015.

Raising Money Within a Religion

Dasvandh is one source of funding within Sikhism. This practice involves Sikhs setting aside 10 percent of their income, or earnings, to contribute to their faith community. However, Sikhs can donate to any community they feel needs the money, such as Khalsa Aid, an international group that helps victims of disasters. Many Sikhs see dasvandh as a religious obligation, or something they are expected to do.

Sikhs also support their faith communities through *tan*, or physical service. Examples of tan include cooking in the langar,

Serving food to the local community is one way Sikhs practice their faith.

Taking Informed Action

Before you read this book, what ideas and opinions did you have about Sikhism? How accurate did they turn out to be? Sometimes, people make snap judgments that set the stage for religious intolerance. Such intolerance is what fuels persecution. Fortunately, learning and sharing knowledge is an opportunity for society to overcome these problems. And you can be part of the solution!

Focus on one feature of all major religions. For example, consider how members of various faiths dress. Find out why certain pieces of clothing are important in Sikhism, Buddhism, Christianity, Hinduism, Islam, and Judaism. Create a chart or a collage that shows your findings. Share what you discover with the people around you—and encourage them to do the same!

Sikhs believe they should spend their lives doing good things for others.

cleaning the gurdwara, or other volunteer opportunities in the local community. Members of Sikhism practice *man*, or mental service, too. Man sometimes takes the form of teaching lessons found within the *Guru Granth Sahib*.

The Survival of Sikhism

Sikh beliefs about giving and a life filled with good works are at the heart of their faith. Sikhism is not the oldest world religion, nor is it the most widely practiced. Nevertheless, it represents a belief system that has endured, or lasted, despite persecution and political conflict. The inner strength that Sikhs have demonstrated since the 16th century has never faded. It is one of many reasons why Sikhism will undoubtedly continue to attract followers for centuries to come.

Communicating Conclusions

Sikhs believe that when they give 10 percent of their earnings, their generosity is ultimately repaid 10 times over. Their kindness helps them achieve good karma and also improves the lives of others. Do you think this is true? What is the potential, or possible, impact of being generous?

As you answer this question, consider using a visual to demonstrate your conclusions. At the top of a piece of poster board, write a few sentences describing an act of giving. Alternately, draw a picture showing such an act.

Underneath your description or image, explain how whoever received help might now be able to help others in turn. Examine how the cycle of giving is ongoing—as well as if or how it eventually helps the person who started it. Share your conclusions with family, friends, or, depending on your beliefs, members of your own faith community.

Think About It

India has a total of 36 states and union territories. According to a recent study by the Indian government, roughly six of them contain most of India's Sikh population. Punjab is among this group and is home to about 75 percent of the nation's Sikhs. What does this data reveal about Sikhism in India? Is it a widespread religion? Or are Sikh populations denser, or more concentrated, in a limited number of areas? What do you think affects Sikh population trends, or patterns, in India?

For More Information

FURTHER READING

Blake, Philip. *My Religion and Me: We Are Sikhs*. London: Hachette Children's Books, 2016.

Coster, Patience and Alex Woolf. *My Life in India*. New York: Cavendish Square Publishing, 2015.

Glossop, Jennifer, and John Mantha (illustrator). *The Kids Book of World Religions*. Toronto: Kids Can Press, Ltd., 2013.

WEB SITES

Khalsa Kids
www.khalsakids.org/index.php
Read articles and play online games that will help you learn more about Sikhism.

SikhNet—Sikh Stories for Children
www.sikhnet.com/stories
Listen to online stories that reflect Sikh beliefs and faith traditions.

GLOSSARY

congregation (kahng-gri-GAY-shun) a group of people assembled for religious worship

deeds (DEEDZ) things that are done

dignity (DIG-nih-tee) the quality or manner that makes a person worthy of honor or respect

equality (ih-KWAH-lih-tee) the right of everyone to be treated the same

fasting (FAST-ing) not eating food for a time

Hinduism (HIN-doo-iz-uhm) a religion and philosophy practiced mainly in India; Hindus worship one or several gods and believe in reincarnation

icons (EYE-kahnz) pictures of holy figures

Islam (iz-LAHM) the religion based on the teachings of Muhammad

oppressors (uh-PRES-urhz) people who use power or authority in a cruel and unfair way

pilgrimages (PIL-grum-ij-ez) trips to a holy place to worship there

pogroms (POH-gruhms) the organized killings of many helpless people usually because of their race or religion

reverence (REV-ur-uhns) honor and respect that is felt or shown

rituals (RICH-oo-uhlz) acts that are always performed in the same way, usually as part of a religious or social ceremony

saints (SAYNTZ) people who have been officially recognized for having lived a very holy life

vices (VISE-iz) immoral or harmful behavior

INDEX